THE
VICTORIANS
BY THE SEA

THE VICTORIANS BY THE SEA

Howard Grey & Graham Stuart

Introduction by Margaret Challen

academy editions·london

st martin's press·new york

Copyright © 1973 by Academy Editions. All rights reserved.

First published in Great Britain in 1973 by Academy Editions,
7 Holland Street, London W.8.

SBN 85670 009 6

First published in the U.S.A. in 1973 by St. Martin's Press Inc.,
175 Fifth Avenue, New York, N.Y. 10010.
Affiliated publisher: Macmillan & Company Limited London -
also at Bombay, Calcutta, Madras and Melbourne.

Printed and bound in Great Britain by University Printing House, Cambridge.

THE VICTORIAN SEASIDE

In the seventeenth century the sea was a reality only for the merchants, sailors and fishermen who depended on it for their livelihoods. Beaches and vistas of water held no particular attraction: all of England looked in on itself, and even fishermen's cottages kept their backs to the sea. It was the search for health, virility and longevity that drew the rich to the coast and changed villages into fashionable resorts, a phenomenon which began at a small harbour named Scarborough, where, in 1626, a chalybeate spring was found, the first mineral spring to be discovered on the coast. A shrewd gentleman from Hull, Dr Wittie, saw commercial possibilities in this novelty. He extended the beneficial effects claimed for bathing in, and drinking, spring water to the water of the sea itself, which in the 1660s he was proclaiming as a cure for gout and worms as well as a tonic for the dissipated and infirm. No-one knows if he himself believed this but Scarborough grew into a popular spa and the doctor no doubt made some profit from the trade. When, some thirty years later, two London physicians published a book naming seawater as a cure for asthma, cancer, consumption, deafness, ruptures, rheumatism, insanity and even failing sexual powers, Scarborough, already established, was in a good position to benefit from the publicity and in the 1730s men and women were seen bathing there 'publicly and frequently'.

The reason for a pilgrimage to the sea was the pursuit of health, as it was for a visit to Bath and Harrogate. The bathe itself was a short but serious ritual. It is known that little Fanny Burney, having booked a machine well in advance, bathed at six one cold November morning. This was not out of eccentricity, she was merely following the advice given by most doctors of the time, who insisted that the best cure was to be had in the coldest water, a theory that sent bathers hurrying to the shore between six and nine, winter and summer, to wait their turn for a machine. Both men and women could bathe naked, if they wished, although doctors often advised the wearing of thin flannel dresses and gauze worsted stockings. The bather was accompanied by one of the professional dippers, usually large, tough working-class women whose original function, like that of their counterparts at the inland spas, had been to help invalids into the water. At the seaside, where being pushed under water was part of the standard treatment, most of the able-bodied also paid for this unnecessary service. Once out in the sea, the bather, after enduring a three-minute dipping, climbed back into the gritty-floored machine which served as a swaying uncomfortable dressing-room while it carried him back to shore.

The rest of the day was taken up with a ride over the sands or a stroll along the jetty (if there was one) to inspect the fishing boats, or with the traditional amusements of the card room or library. Newer seaside resorts did their best to satisfy the social requirements of the well-to-do by providing library, rotunda and assembly rooms, but these trappings of themselves could not create the bustling atmosphere that characterized the long-standing Scarborough or Bath. Arriving at Weymouth in 1789 Fanny Burney lamented, "I have here a very good parlour but dull, from its aspect. Nothing but the sea at Weymouth affords any life or spirit". Yet the pleasures of the sea seemed greater where social distractions were few for she continued later, "I am delighted with the soft air and soft footing upon the sands and stroll up and down them morning, noon and night". Wide esplanades and elegant, large-windowed houses facilitated the enjoyment of a walk by the sea and a view of the sea — still part of the seaside ritual today.

The pleasures of breathing the pure and bracing air of the sea were available almost solely to the rich. Unplanned industry and housing had devoured much urban green and open space and for the poor there was no escape from the constant smoke, dirt and smells from open sewers which, unpleasant all year round, made town life dangerously unhealthy and almost unbearable in summer. The annual exodus of the wealthy to resorts or country houses left the cities in summer to the working classes. Some of the organized industries like the mines, potteries and cotton mills, gave their workers holidays of as much as a week, but, with travel across land still prohibitively expensive, slow and uncomfortable, they stayed at home and indulged in a more practical release, drinking beer and gin.

1

2

3. Anon. Clacton promenade, c. 1903

At the beginning of the nineteenth century war made the sea the object of national attention. With invasion expected the south coast offered more menace, excitement and romance than at any time since the Armada. Cannons were mounted at strategic points (they can still be seen at Hythe), the fleet waited majestically outside the harbour, ready to set sail for battle, the dockyards of Southampton and Portsmouth were crowded with vessels. The war, as Thackeray tells us, had the air of a social event: "Margate packets were sailing everyday, filled with men of fashion and ladies of note, on their way to Brussels and Ghent. People were going not so much to a war as to a fashionable tour". Army encampments on the coast filled resorts with dashing soldiers and officers. Brighton was in its heyday with Prinny and his racy playmates in the forefront of fashion and even less popular places like Hastings and Eastbourne began to attract more lively society.

The excitement was temporary, followed by the usual post-war depression, but prospects for resorts all over Britain revived with the invention of two revolutionary modes of transportation, the steamboat and the railway. Steam-powered boats began to run in 1817; the first railway, between Stockton and Darlington, was opened to the public in 1823. To industrialists and agents the steamboat meant greatly improved commercial connections and it was not long before its tourist

1. Anon. On the rocks, Hastings, c. 1900

2. Anon. On the beach at Yarmouth, c. 1900

5. Anon. Dragging in the boats, Chessil, 1872

potential was realised. Steamers began to run between London and Margate, Newcastle and Whitby and other major resorts and cities, and eventually ran between Hythe and the Isle of Wight, and Fleetwood and Douglas on the Isle of Man. The mid-nineteenth century was, nevertheless, the age of the railway. In its early days fares were high, and the steam engine with its great power and speed seemed to many a frightening affair. Yet the novelty was so attractive that the first London to Brighton train in 1841 had six engines and fifty-seven carriages and was filled with nearly 2000 passengers, who had no complaint about their five-hour journey. This successful run proved that every major resort would be incomplete without its own railway station and by 1850 there were 6,621 miles of track carrying 73,000,000 passengers a year, many of them holiday makers. Lower fares, special excursion tickets for families and parties of people, and a general rise in the standard of living, meant that a different sort of person could now afford an occasional holiday at the coast — the railway had democratized the seaside resort.

4. Anon. The Estuary near Pont Dlu, 1888 (Previous pages)

Places previously protected from an invasion of the lower classes by their isolation were so no more, and many genteel middle-class families fled to quieter places such as Walton-on-the-Naze, Bognor, Torquay, Teignmouth, the Isle of Wight (Queen Victoria's own choice) and little villages in Wales, or the suburbs of resorts, Hove, Ramsgate, and St Anne's. During the month or more they stayed there ladies read quantities of books from the circulating library, sketched or hunted for seashells to add to their collections while children dug sandcastles or scrambled among the rocks. At weekends or during their short holidays, fathers played cricket with their sons and took the family boating. Even in these undeveloped resorts, men and women still dressed in strict accordance with fashion, not for comfort or convenience. That unyielding, and to our eyes incongruous, garment, the crinoline hoop, can be seen in photographs or paintings from photographs of the period, like Dyce's *Pegwell Bay* and Frith's *Ramsgate Sands.* Long skirts dragged in sand and water — only children and fisherwomen hitched them up — and men were politely attired in jacket, waistcoat, tie and hat. At the more sophisticated resorts the situation was extreme with "Ladies of fashion", as one magazine reported, taking "no less than from forty to sixty dresses for one season by the seaside". Even day trippers wore their Sunday best.

People now bathed for pleasure and sat all day on the beach. Those seeking medicinal cures had left Margate and Brighton for Bournemouth and what used to be a private, regulated activity was now a public frolic or an embarrassing ritual. Although men bathed naked, women used the ugly, heavy flannel dresses designed to be worn only by the shy or invalid a century before. Loose and unbelted, they were now small protection in the crowded waters nearer the shore. Bourgeois modesty had taken hold of public opinion and the *Observer* in the summer of 1856 found the immoral scenes on the beaches of Ramsgate and Margate "this year worse than ever", blaming the conditions on cheap fares "which has filled these watering places to over-flowing, and the class of visitors, which is perhaps lower than usual . . . The water is black with bathers; should the sea be rather rough the females do not venture beyond the surf, and lay themselves on their backs, waiting for the coming waves, with their bathing dresses in a most dégagée style. The waves come, and, in the majority of instances, not only cover the fair bathers, but literally carry their dresses up to their neck, so that, as far as decency is concerned, they might as well be without any dresses at all . . . In fact, it is looked upon much as a scene at a play would be, as the gentlemen are there with their opera glasses, bandying criticisms . . . The portion of the beach allotted to the men is crowded with well-dressed females, or, in other words, ladies, who calmly look on without a blush or even a giggle, and who seem to be much amused at what is going forward . . . How is it that ladies who are so very delicate in London, should, when they arrive at Ramsgate, throw off all pretentions to modesty and decency, as they do their shawls and wrappers?" Complaints had been heard before. In 1800 the *Observer* reported that "the indecency of numerous naked men bathing in the sea close to the ladies' machines, and under the windows of the principal houses at most of the watering places, had been long complained of . . ." But it was not until the middle of the century, when the authorities, sharing the self-righteous middle-class mood, felt that their moral duty to the masses demanded the establishment and enforcement of regulations prescribing the distance to be set between male and female bathing machines and requiring men to wear trunks, and women to wear drawers and belts. If this sport was spoiled high spirits soon found other outlets in listening to the military bands and barrel organs, singing and laughing with Uncle Bones and the Nigger Minstrels, walking along the pier (nearly every self-respecting resort had a pleasure pier by the 1860s), showing off your new clothes or buying little souvenirs, and, best souvenir of all, having your picture taken by the local photographer. Even the less sober of the middle classes began to find these jostling, noisy crowds too much for them. As they began to move away the authorities panicked, begging railway companies to put up their fares to discourage the trippers. But the poor were getting richer and their money was missed. Brighton, Eastbourne, and Bournemouth began to suffer, their growth rate dropped dramatically, and in the end they gave in. The customer, they conceded, is always right, and you couldn't always choose your customer.

Resorts which had grudgingly accepted the working and lower middle class trippers now set out to attract them. The Bank Holiday Act of 1871 gave new impetus to the trend; lodging houses opened in growing numbers, food stalls selling fried fish, pies and ice cream arrived from London for the season to compete with the oyster shellers and the cold meat shops. The air was as loud as ever with brass bands, Punch and Judy, and the new Pierrots. Not everyone wanted such blatant entertainment. Self-improvement was much encouraged by the Victorians, and keen young clerks and shop assistants newly released by the Bank Holidays, strove to raise their status by taking part in middle class activities. Apart from reading or attending scientific lectures at the library there were more active pleasures to pursue. They looked for local colour in the remote fishing villages of Devon, Cornwall and Wales, sketched or photographed picturesque scenes of the fishing boats and natives. They joined history, natural history and archaeology clubs and organised walking tours, a well-meaning devotee of which admitted: "I am loth to commend a visit to the seaside as it is generally paid. To be sure, you have the sea, which is ever old and young, a changing and yet constant friend. And you have the beach, on which you may set fresh footprints with a sense of traversing virgin ground after each waning of the water . . . but the style and shallow fashion of these (watering places) is, to my mind, monotonously oppressive. There is often a sort of toyshop look about them, and a donkey-driving, band-listening, telescopic weariness of pertinacity which is soon tiresome . . . If you want to combine sea air and exercise in a short holiday, take a walking tour by the seaside, and use the frequented watering-places only as stations in which to rest for a night or for a meal". He goes on, with all the Victorian sense of excitement about exploration, to suggest walking tours of several weeks in the Swiss Alps or even in America.

For less stimulating reasons the continental resorts, such as Dieppe, Boulogne and Ostend were beginning to syphon off the wealthier families. The attractions were the reportedly safer bathing (there were many fatal swimming accidents off the British coast in the early 70s) and a chance to escape from their own working class. No doubt they would have escaped sooner, but upheavals on the French political scene kept them away until the latter half of the century. Places like Trouville and Le Touquet became like English colonies, far too anglicised to be called French.

Those who spent their holidays there were not really missed back in England, except perhaps by the larger, more expensive hotels. The working man was finding new freedoms in paid holidays (though this was not wide-spread till the early 20th century) and individual transportation. The bicycle was a humble beginning, but young men and women of the 80s and 90s must have been thrilled at the independence it offered them. The new invention brought a new freedom for women. For this one activity they were granted the right to wear trousers, or rather bloomers, still unacceptable for playing tennis or hockey. Only bathers revealed a bit of stockinged leg, and most of these daring souls were still camera shy, possibly because their costumes were made of unsuitable materials such as cotton which clung revealingly to the figure when wet. Once women no longer wore corsets underneath, as they had done in the 70s and 80s, the walk to the bathing machine or continental tent must have been embarrassing. In spite of this, mixed bathing was introduced at Bexhill soon after 1900 and by 1914 it was almost universal.

This new sexual freedom is reflected in some of the photographs by Paul Martin. With his 'detective' camera hidden in an ordinary canvas bag he managed to take pictures of lovers lying on the beach in each others arms as unselfconsciously as they do today, ladies hanging ungracefully to the rope of their bathing machine, and hoisting their skirts out of the path of the waves. With fast shutter speeds and film the photographer no longer needed the consent of his subjects, and was able to capture situations just as they happened. The "candid" photographer coincided with already apparent trends towards a less formal and hide-bound society, trends perhaps more marked at seaside resorts than anywhere else. The new style included bed & breakfast lodging, tearooms and cheap cafés, looser, simpler clothes (though everyone still wore hats), amusement arcades with their new "What the butler saw" slot machines. At night strings of lights glittered along the promenade and decorated that ultimate in seaside fantasy, the pier. Unlike the early days of the watering place (as it continued to be called) social life for visitors was centred on the beach rather than the town. It followed cheaper and more flexible patterns, which suited the worker better than the socialite. Eighteenth century visitors had demanded a busy, organised and monotonous round of townlife amusements similar to that offered at the spas. The 19th century workers wanted a great variety of amusements, music they could sing to, shows to make them laugh and enjoy the sea air, to forget their dreary cramped offices, dirty streets and noisy factories, to do what they wanted when they wanted.

7. F. M. Sutcliffe. Fishing boats at Whitby, 1885-90

6. Valentine. Filey Bay, 1895

9. Peter Henry Emerson. *Great Yarmouth Harbour,* 1890

8. Colonel Stuart Wortley. *Towards Evening,* c. 1865

10

11

12. Anon. *The Castle and Bridge, Inverness*, 1868

10. Anon. Caernarvon Castle, North Wales, 1885

11. James Valentine & Co. Caernarvon Castle, c.1895

13

14

15. F. M. Sutcliffe. Whitby, c. 1890

3. Frith of Reigate. Newlyn harbour, 1902

4. P. H. Emerson. *Old Hulks,* 1890

Frank Meadows Sutcliffe (1853-1941) lived and worked as a professional photographer in Whitby, Yorkshire from 1875, producing carte-de-visite and cabinet portrait photographs. In the late 80s, influenced by the famous advocate of naturalistic photography Dr. Peter Henry Emerson, he began taking pictures of life in the farming areas and fishing ports of Yorkshire. With good outdoor light the new fast-dry gelatine plates gave perfectly clear images of static objects, and Sutcliffe demonstrated beautifully that posed people do not have to lose all spontaneity of expression.

16, 17. F. M. Sutcliffe. Fishergirls at Whitby, 1885-90

9. F. M. Sutcliffe. *An interested group at Whitby*, 1885-90

8. F. M. Sutcliffe. *Fisherman and his granddaughters*, 1885-90

20. F. M. Sutcliffe. Urchins at Whitby, c. 1890 (overleaf)

21. F. M. Sutcliffe. Fisherman's family at Whitby, c. 1890

22. F. M. Sutcliffe. Fishergirls at Whitby, c. 1890

23, 24. F. M. Sutcliffe. Fisherlassies at Whitby, c. 1890

19th century Whitby was a little East-coast fishing harbour about twenty miles from the popular coastal spa, Scarborough. It had a distinguished history as a centre of the boat-building industry until iron boats began to supercede traditional wooden constructions, and a continuous tradition of fishing going back a thousand years. The Whitby boatyards even developed their own flat-bottomed fishing boats called "cobles" which were specially suited to the shallows and shelving beaches of the Yorkshire coast. Sutcliffe's pictures of the town and its inhabitants recall none of the precarious nature of fishing in those days, rather they show the more positive aspects of this integrated if primitive community, perhaps the last generation of children to follow unquestioningly in their parents' footsteps.

25

26

29. F. M. Sutcliffe. Fishergirls by the quay, Whitby, c. 1890

Previous pages:
25, 26, 27. F. M. Sutcliffe. Fisherfolk and "cobles" at Whitby, c. 1890

28. F. M. Sutcliffe. Mending the nets, Whitby, c. 1890

30. F. M. Sutcliffe. On the beach at low tide, Whitby, c. 1890

31, 32, 33. F. M. Sutcliffe. *Sunshine and Fog at Whitby*, c. 1880-85

36. *Jas Linton at Newhaven,* c. 1845

David Octavius Hill, a successful artist, started using the calotype process in 1843 as an aid to painting a group portrait. He collaborated with Robert Adamson, who was already a practising photographer, and their combined technical and artistic skills produced remarkable results in portraiture, and in a famous series of genre pictures taken at the fishing ports of Newhaven and St. Andrews.

34. *St. Andrew's Fishmarket,* c. 1845-8

35. *Newhaven Fishwives,* c. 1845-8

37. Anon. *Waiting for the Boats*, 1865

38. Francis Bedford.

Fishing Boats at Newlyn, 1863

40. F. M. Sutcliffe.

Fisherlassies at Whitby,

c. 1890 (Overleaf)

39. D. O. Hill and R. Adamson. St. Andrews, c. 1845

41

42

43. Valentine & Co. St. Ives, c. 1895

41. Anon. The beach at Hastings, c. 1870

42. Anon. *Southport Cockler Women,* c. 1897

44. Valentine & Co. *In the Digey, St. Ives*, c. 1895

45. Valentine & Co. *The Oldest House in St. Ives,* c. 1895

This old Cornish town is not only the head-quarters of the pilchard fishery, but also the centre of a very beautiful district, more than one point of which may claim to be considered as an independent watering-place. St. Ives itself has a splendid beach of silver sand, a conspicuous promontory, known as the Island, and a line of "towans" or grass-grown sandhills; then, not far off, is a wealth of the splendid cliff, cove, and cavern scenery so characteristic of Cornwall. The town lies nestling under low hills on the very skirt of St. Ives Bay and, with the blue sky and ocean, the green tints of the shallows, and the sparkle of the bright yellow sandy shore, forms altogether a picture of uncommon beauty. St. Ives is picturesquely built on broken ground, and the old streets in the lower part are narrow and crooked enough to be almost mediaeval in effect, while the heights above are studded with handsome modern residences. The rocky peninsula, known as the Island, lies to the north of the town, and on it is a battery commanding a fine view.
From **Round the Coast,** 1895

46

47

48. Francis Bedford. The trading ship Emily at Torquay, c. 1865

46. Anon. *The Channel Fleet in the Firth of Forth*, 1859

47. Francis Bedford. *Beaumaris. The Training Ship Clio*, c. 1875

49, 51. W. H. Fox Talbot. Sailing craft, c. 1845

50. Anon. *The Champion at Portsmouth*, 1849

William Henry Fox Talbot, a wealthy landowner born in 1800, began experimenting with photography in 1833, and in 1835 produced the earliest surviving negative. Spurred on by Daguerre's claims to have invented the first photographic process (Daguerreotypes were positive only) he published his own negative/positive process. In 1840 he managed to reduce the necessary exposure from about one hour to two or three minutes by his discovery of a 'latent' image which could be developed with gallo nitrate of silver. He patented and published this new method, the Calotype or Talbotype, in 1841.

From 1843 to 1847 Talbot and his assistant, Nikolaas Henneman, working from his photographic establishment in Reading, produced portraits, genre and landscape photos - anything which would or could stay still for three minutes together. Unfortunately, the fixing processes were not adequate to prevent the images fading with time, but many taken in this early period are clear enough to reveal Talbot's aesthetic as well as technical talents.

52. The London Stereoscopic Company. *The East India Docks,* 1895

53. P. H. Emerson. *The Flood Tide,* Yarmouth, 1890

54. Anon. *The Thames at Greenwich,* 1866

55. Francis Bedford. Bristol, c. 1870

56. Francis Bedford. *Bristol. The Sparrow,* c. 1870

57

58

57. Francis Bedford. *Sidmouth from the West*, c. 1880

58. Anon. *Harvesting at Ilfracombe*, c. 1906

59. Paul Martin. *Watching a Pleasure Steamer, Jersey*, 1893

60. P. H. Emerson. *The Ferry, Yarmouth*, 1890

61. F. S. Mann. *Ship Aground at Hastings*, c. 1870 (Overleaf)

62.   Frank M. Good.   The Needles, Isle of Wight, 1870

63.   James Valentine. Off Douglas, Isle of Man, 1875

64

65

66

67

69. Francis Bedford. Sidmouth, 1868

68. Francis Bedford. Ilfracombe, 1875

The idea of seeing the sea - of being near it - watching its changes by sunrise, sunset, moonlight ,and noon day   in calm, perhaps in storm
· fills and satisfies my mind. I shall be discontented at nothing.
August, 1839
Have you forgotten the sea by this time, E? Is it grown dim in your mind or can you still see it, dark, blue, and green, and foam-white,
and hear it roaring roughly when the wind is high, or rushing softly when it is calm . . .
October, 1839
Charlotte Bronte. From her letters

70. Frith of Reigate. *Exmouth Sands,* 1892

71. Frith of Reigate. Bridlington, 1898

72. Anon. Weymouth, 1906

73

74

5. Anon. Clacton, 1906

, 74. Paul Martin. *Yarmouth Sands,* 1892

76. C. and P. *Exmouth Sands*, 1892

77. Paul Martin. Searching for Cockles, c. 1894

78. Francis Bedford. Penmaenmawr, c. 1870

77

78

As Justice Shallow might say, Blackpool has two piers, and everything handsome about her. Both the piers are large, the north one is the more select, and the south the more popular - just a penny pier where dancing goes on all day in the summer. In this Lancashire watering-place there are theatres, a "Grand Opera House", numerous concert halls, an aquarium, a circus, a menagerie, fine winter gardens, and other places of public assemblies, where concerts, fireworks, and all sorts of entertainments will be found duly provided. The Royal Palace Gardens, commonly known as Raikes Hall, seem to be the most popular favourite among these resorts. The promenade is lighted by electricity, and has an electric tramway. Not to be left behind in any respect, Blackpool now has an Eiffel Tower of its own, which looks down upon a busy scene of enjoyment that suggests a fair rather than a seaside resort . . . Blackpool is a popular resort in every sense of the term; people visit it with the avowed intention of enjoying themselves to their hearts' content; and that they are successful in this respect is proclaimed by the mighty crowds that flock thither season after season, never tiring of the almost uproarious merriment that characterizes the famous Lancashire watering-place.

From **Round the Coast,** 1895

80

80. Anon. *Blackpool. Donkeys,* 1901

81. Anon. Blackpool, 1896

79. Frith of Reigate. Weymouth, 1896

82. Frith of Reigate. Blackpool, 1896 (Overleaf)

83

84

85. Frith of Reigate. Lynmouth, 1906

83. Paul Martin. *The Artist at Appledore,* 1894

84. Anon. La Panne, 1902

86. Paul Martin. *Trippers Caught by a Wave, Yarmouth,* 1892

Paul Martin (1864-1942) was the first 'candid cameraman' in the modern style. While serving his apprenticeship to a London firm of wood engravers working for newspapers he realised, with great foresight, that the half-tone block would eventually put engravers like himself out of work, and in 1884 he started taking photographs in his spare time. He hid his detective camera (originally designed to be used by the police) in an ordinary-looking bag with a hole just big enough for the lens to poke through thereby contriving to catch his subjects unawares. By the early 1900s he was established as a free-lance photographer in the Strand, and had taken some of his best pictures of London street life and the seaside at Yarmouth.

87. Paul Martin. *Hanging out the Washing, Hastings,* c. 1892

88. Paul Martin. *Children swinging. Hastings,* c. 1892

87

88

90.   Paul Martin. Hastings, c. 1894

89.   Paul Martin. *Urchins at Hastings,* c. 1894

91. Anon. *An Averted Disaster*, 1906

92. Anon. *Paddling at Scarborough*, 1904

93. Frith of Reigate. *A Real Mermaid*, 1897

94. Anon. *Sunday School Outing at Southend*, 1905

95. J. Reeves. *Family Group at Hastings*, 1897

96. Anon. *Tunnel Beach, Ilfracombe,* 1856

97.   Anon. *Sandcastles at Sidmouth*, 1905

98, 99. Paul Martin. *Paddling at Yarmouth* 1892

100. Paul Martin. Yarmouth, 1892

101. Anon. Yarmouth, 1907

102. Frith of Reigate. *Granny's Teeth*, 1904

103. Francis Bedford. *Pensarn Beach*, c. 1870 (Overleaf)

104. Francis Bedford. Rhyl, c. 1890

The town of Rhyl, like most of the Welsh watering-places, is of very recent growth, and not many years ago there was no town at all, but merely a few fishermen's huts upon the shore. The sands, which are extensive enough to give the full benefit of ozone to those who avail themselves of its health-giving properties, form an excellent bathing-ground, entirely free from danger. Hence Rhyl has become noted for the number of children that visit it, and these little ones find an inexhaustible fund of pleasure on its beach. There is a splendid promenade, about a mile in length, and of great width, also a fine promenade pier.
From **Round the Coast,** 1895

105. Anon. *Donkey Travel,* 1869

106. George Dean. *Douglas,* 1865

107

108

109. Anon. *Clacton Pier*, 1903

This new and rapidly rising seaside resort is pleasantly situated on the Essex coast, sixty-eight miles from London . . . For cleanliness, firmness, and extent, the sands of Clacton-on-Sea cannot be excelled; for they are a perennial source of delight to the children, and for visitors generally they form a safe and pleasant promenade for miles each way. Bathing is safe at all time, the sands being firm, and sloping gently out to deep water. One of the chief attractions of Clacton is its fine pier, which has now been so much enlarged and improved, that as a promenade there are very few similar constructions which can equal it.
From **Round the Coast**, 1895

107. Anon. *Clacton. Arrival of Trippers*, 1903

108. Anon. *Southwold*, 1904

110. Anon. *Group at Fairlight,* Hastings, 1856

111. Anon. *Afternoon Relaxations,* 1875

Following pages:
112. Francis Bedford. *Llandudno. The Happy Valley,* 1868

113. Anon. Clacton. The Pierrots, c. 1900

114. Anon. Margate, 1903

115. Anon. Baby Show, Margate, 1908

112

113

114

115

116

117

118. Paul Martin. *Punch and Judy Show at Ilfracombe,* 1894

116. Paul Martin. *Yarmouth. Crowds Listening to a Concert,* 1892

117. Anon. Refreshment house, Land's End, c. 1880

119. Anon. Uncle Bones, c. 1900

20. Francis Bedford. Clovelly, 1870

21. Anon. Clacton, 1906

122. Francis Bedford. *Rhyl. The Parade,* c. 1875

. . . There are a great many donkey carriages - large vehicles drawn by a pair of donkeys; bath-chairs with invalid ladies; refreshment rooms in great numbers - a place where everybody seems to be a transitory guest, nobody at home. The main street leads directly down to the seashore along which there is an elevated embankment, with a promenade on the top, and seats and the toll of a penny . . . people riding on donkeys, children digging with little wooden spades and donkey carriages far out on the sands a pleasant and breezy drive.
Nathaniel Hawthorne. From his journal, 1856

123. Anon. *Donkey Rides at Scarborough,* 1908

124. Anon. *Donkey Men. Southend,* 1908

126. Anon. Snapshot, 1899

127. Anon. Family group, Freshwater, 1871

125. Anon. Clacton Pier, 1903 (Previous pages)

128

129

130. Paul Martin. *Bathing at Yarmouth,* 1892

Image to yourself a small, snug, wooden chamber, fixed on a wheel-carriage, having a door at each end, and, on each side, a little window above, a bench below. The bather, ascending into this apartment by wooden steps, shuts himself in, and begins to undress; while the attendant yokes a horse to the end next to the sea, and draws the carriage forward, till the surface of the water is on a level with the floor of the dressing-room then he moves and fixes the horse to the other end. The person within, being stripped, opens the door to the seaward, where he finds the guide ready, and plunges headlong into the water. After having bathed he re-ascends into the apartment by the steps which had been shifted for that purpose, and puts on his clothes at his leisure, while the carriage is drawn back again up on the dry land; so that he has nothing further to do but to open the door and come down as he went up ... The guides who attend the ladies in the water are of their own sex; and they and the female bathers have a dress of flannel for the sea; nay, they are provided with other conveniences for the support of decorum. A certain number of the machines are fitted with tilts, that project from the seaward ends of them, so as to screen the bathers from the view of all persons whatsoever.
From **The Expedition of Humphrey Clinker,** Tobias Smollett, 1771

128. Anon. Broadstairs, 1904

129. Anon. Felixstowe, 1902

131. G. W. Wilson. *Clamshell Cave and Herdsman Island. Staffa,* c. 1870

132. G. W. Wilson. Skye, c. 1870